ACCOUNTING FOR SMALL BUSINESS

Know the Processes and Terminologies Involved in Maintaining Your Company Financials

Stephanie Horne

Small business isn't for the faint of heart. It's for the brave, the patient, & the persistent. It's for the overcomer.

—ANONYMOUS

CONTENTS

Accounting For Small Business 1
Contents 3
About The Author 6
Accounting For 7
Small Business 7
Accounting For Small Business 8
Business Structure 9
Business Bookkeeping Principals 10
Bookkeeping Services & sKILLS 11
Business Plan Advice 12
Small Business Tax Services 13
Business Planner 14
Online Business Bank Account 15
Business Structure 17
Sole Proprietor Business Structure 18
Partnerships 19
Limited Liability Companies 20
Corporations 21
S Corporations 22
Sound Bookkeeping Principles 24
Sound Bookkeeping Principles for Businesses 25
Developing a Bookkeeping System 27
Contact Us if You Need Help 30
Business Bank Account 31
Online Business Bank Account 32
Online Accounting Software 33
Online Accounting Apps 34
Business Skills and Bookkeeping Services 35
3 Critical Accounting Strengths 37

Business Organization	44
Summary	49
Business Plan Advice	50
Automate Books	51
Bookkeeping Tips	52
Increase Efficiency	56
Small Business Tax Services	57
Small Business Tax Services	58
Business Tax Incentive Benefits	60
Business Planner	63
Business Planners For All	64
Functionality	65
Use Colors	66
Bookmarks	67
Getting Started	68
Additional Resources	70
Notes	72

ABOUT THE AUTHOR

Stephanie has a passion for helping people to improve their lives both personally and financially by learning new financial and personal self-help tools.

Her own personal journey has led to compiling this book that reveals many simple financial techniques that anyone can apply immediately for a powerful, positive money and business success transformation.

By the end of this book, you'll know how the need for personal self-improvement and knowledge determines the actions we should take moving forward for a better financial future.

ACCOUNTING FOR SMALL BUSINESS

Understanding the Financial Process

Don't ever let your business get ahead of the financial side of your business. Accounting, accounting, accounting. Know your numbers.
—Tilman J. Fertitta

WHEN DOING YOUR ACCOUNTING FOR small business, how well do you understand the terminology and processes involved in maintaining your business financials?

As a small business owner, it is very important to understand how accounting & bookkeeping tie into your everyday operations.

Keeping track of your profits and deductible expenses will indicate how well your business is doing and what you need to do to improve.

Even if you are able to hire a bookkeeper or accountant to handle your finances, it's good to have a handle on the basics of small business finances.

ACCOUNTING FOR SMALL BUSINESS

When thinking about your small business accounting, there are many factors to consider. Like, what kind of business structure do you have?

This will make a difference on the different types of business bookkeeping principals your will be using as well as the different types of business skills and bookkeeping services you may need.

This will also be important with regards to setting up a business plan how you will go about handling your business taxes.

BUSINESS STRUCTURE

Choosing the right business structure can be a difficult task when doing accounting for small business.

To assist taxpayers who are starting their own business, the Treasury Department releases a fact sheet that lists the differences between the most common forms of business entities.

They advise that each business structure should be evaluated from a tax, liability and record keeping perspective.

The fact sheet summarizes some of the important traits of the four most commonly utilized business entities operating in the U.S. today:

1. Sole proprietorships
2. Partnerships
3. Corporations, including Subchapter S corporations (S-corps)
4. Limited liability companies (LLCs)

BUSINESS BOOKKEEPING PRINCIPALS

As a small business owner, it is very important to understand how accounting & bookkeeping principals tie into your everyday accounting for small business operations.

Keeping track of your profits and deductible expenses will indicate how well your business is doing and what you need to do to improve.

Even if you are able to hire a bookkeeper or accountant to handle your finances, it's good to have a handle on the basics of small business finances.

BOOKKEEPING SERVICES & SKILLS

If you are asking what business skills and bookkeeping services have to do with each other, then you are asking a great question that I would love to answer.

Many years ago during an intense conversation with one of my mentors she advised me to always remember that there is only one constant; and that constant is that everything around us are changing.

That is so true. You just have to think of all the changes to the tax code every year to realize why I, as an Enrolled Agent and bookkeeper, regard continuous learning as one of the most critical business skills and bookkeeping services for business owners and business professionals.

BUSINESS PLAN ADVICE

Accountants are forced to handle a growing number of accounts, but few of them are looking for ways to improve efficiency.

Ken Brown, the executive director of the IFO, said that their unwillingness to adapt is creating a massive backlog for accounts payable professionals.

He said that even though many invoices are prepared electronically, the majority of bookkeeping and accounts payable professionals enter the data manually.

A surprising number of businesses still receive paper invoices. Brown said that 27% of businesses receive 90% or more of their invoices on paper, while only 9% receive an equivalent number of electronic invoices.

Here are some business plan & bookkeeping tips every bookkeeping and accounts payable professional should consider.

SMALL BUSINESS TAX SERVICES

The Sonoma County Economic Development Board is trying to expand the tax credits available to local businesses.

They have introduced some new tax credits that were made available under the California Competes bill, which was passed by Governor Brown.

Under the new program, business owners would be eligible for up to $31 million in tax credits. However, many companies may need the assistance of local tax experts to navigate the new systems.

BUSINESS PLANNER

There are many independent business contractors who use planners to keep track of important dates and client information to have within arm's reach to reference back to.

So to all of the business owners or employees who only rely solely on your brain, or the calendar in your cell phone; it's time to stop!

If your cell phone dies, or the awful chance that you misplace it without backing it up to the iCloud, you will lose all of that valuable information in the blink of an eye!

Save yourself the hassle, and invest in a hard-copy planner that organizes all of the new incoming information. It can easily be edited and updated, and in the long run, save you extraordinary amounts of precious time.

ONLINE BUSINESS BANK ACCOUNT

Opening an online business bank account that is separate from your personal financial assets is one of the first steps you should take when starting a new business.

It is very important that you maintain separate personal & company assets and stay away from what is known as co-mingling as a business owner when doing your accounting for small business banking.

This is to ensure that you will not have any problems and will be more audit proof when it comes to doing your taxes.

.

BUSINESS STRUCTURE

Find the Right Entity for Your Business

You have to work on the business first before it works for you.
—Idowu Koynikan

CHOOSING THE RIGHT BUSINESS structure for your business can feel like a difficult task. To assist taxpayers who are starting their own company, the treasury department releases a fact sheet that lists the differences between the most common forms of business entities.

The Treasury advises that each business structure should be evaluated from a tax, liability and record keeping perspective.

The Treasury's fact sheet summarizes some of the important traits of the four most commonly utilized business entities operating in the U.S. today:

1. Sole proprietorships
2. Partnerships
3. Corporations, including Subchapter S corporations (S-corps)
4. Limited liability companies (LLCs)

SOLE PROPRIETOR BUSINESS STRUCTURE

The sole proprietorship is one of the most common types of business structure entities, in part because it is easily formed. The owner of a sole proprietorship is personally liable for the debts and other obligations of the entity.

Additionally, a sole proprietor must pay self-employment tax and, since taxes are not withheld, must make quarterly estimated tax payments. Generally, a sole proprietor files Form 1040, Schedule C on their personal income tax return.

PARTNERSHIPS

A partnership is a popular "pass-through" entity organized by two or more individuals.

Income, credit, deductions, profits and losses pass through the partnership to the partners, who must report the information on their individual income tax returns (Form 1040).

No tax is paid at the partnership level although a Form 1065, U.S. Return of Partnership Income, is filed in the name of the partnership. Since no tax is withheld at the entity level, partners must make quarterly estimated tax payments

LIMITED LIABILITY COMPANIES

The LLC enjoyed a meteoric rise to popularity in the 1990s. The LLC is a creature of state law and every state, as well as the District of Columbia, has adopted statutory provisions governing the formation and operation of LLCs.

The LLC is popular because, like a corporation, its members enjoy limited personal liability for the debts and other obligations of the entity, and like a partnership, it is a pass-through entity business structure.

In order to be an LLC you will need to file a legal LLC operating agreement.

All items of income, profits, loss, deductions, and credits pass through to individual members. In general, a LLC can have a single member or multiple members. A single member LLC is generally taxed, for federal tax purposes, as a sole proprietorship and a multi-member LLC is taxed as a partnership.

CORPORATIONS

Like LLCs, the formation of a corporation business structure is governed by state law. Generally, corporations pay tax at both the state and federal levels.

A corporation files Form 1120, U.S. Corporation Income Tax Return, and pays tax at rates. Corporate earnings that are distributed to shareholders as dividends are taxed at individual rates on shareholders' individual income tax returns.

However, shareholders are shielded from personal liability as liability for the debts and other obligations of the entity rest with the corporation.

If you would like to set your business up as a Corporation, you can find do it yourself articles of incorporation online.

S CORPORATIONS

A Subchapter S corporation (commonly referred to as an S-Corp) is a legal entity that follows state law like a corporation and the shareholders have only limited liability.

However, it is similar, in some respects, to a partnership because income passes through the S-Corp to individual shareholders, who report income and other items on their individual income tax returns.

To be treated as an S-Corp for federal tax purposes, a corporation must file Form 2553, Election by a Small Business Corporation.

An S-Corp files Form 1120S, U.S. Corporation Income Tax Return for an S Corporation. This is an information return only. The income "flows through" to each shareholder's individual income tax return.

If you'd like a more detailed explanation of the strengths and weaknesses of a particular business entity, please contact my office

SOUND BOOKKEEPING PRINCIPLES

Key Elements of Running a Business

Behind every good business is a great bookkeeper.
—ANONYMOUR

IN ORDER TO MANAGE YOUR COMPANY'S finances, you need to practice sound bookkeeping and accounting principles. All business owners should follow these following tips.

Are you one of the few business owners that review your businesses financial statements every month? Research indicates that the majority of small business owners do not practice sound bookkeeping principles as they do not realize the value of understanding their financial statements.

However, practicing sound bookkeeping principles is an essential element of running a business.

If you are reluctant to record your financial transactions, we urge you to take the time to understand the importance and implement a system that is easy to follow.

SOUND BOOKKEEPING PRINCIPLES FOR BUSINESSES

Recording financial transactions can be a very tedious process for active businesses. However, there are a number of reasons that bookkeeping is extremely important:

- You keep track of your bills so that you don't face late fees or order cancellations.
- You remember to send invoices for goods and services that you have delivered.
- You keep better track of outstanding liabilities, which keeps you from getting too deeply in debt.
- You will have a better idea of your available capital, which will allow you to allocate it more prudently.

Practicing sound bookkeeping principles is important to remain financially solvent and track expenditures.

However, many businesses have difficulty finding the time needed to implement it properly. They will need to develop a system that allows them to keep track of their finances as efficiently as possible.

DEVELOPING A BOOKKEEPING SYSTEM

You may run into some challenges with bookkeeping. Businesses need to find a way to keep track of their transactions efficiently to avoid any challenges they may face. Consider the following tips to develop a bookkeeping system.

Learn the Basics

You don't need to be a rocket scientist to learn the basics of bookkeeping. Petaluma companies can figure them out pretty easily after taking a course or reading a book on the topic. This blog also provides plenty of material to help you get started.

There are a number of subtle rules that you will need to learn, but they all revolve around the fundamental rule of accounting.

After learning this rule and the way debits and credits work, you will be able to start implementing a bookkeeping strategy.

Organize Your Records

It is imperative that you keep track of all financial records. Make sure that the following documents are carefully organized:

- Invoices from suppliers to manage accounts payable
- Records of work completed
- Banking and credit card statements
- Receipts for any payments

- Accurate records for tax liabilities

It is a good idea to retain both physical and electronic records of all financial transactions.

You will need them to cross-reference your financial records for discrepancies, so make sure that you save them even if you believe the information is redundant.

Invest in Bookkeeping Software

QuickBooks and other accounting software can streamline the bookkeeping process. You can purchase a standard version of QuickBooks for about $250.

It is well worth the investment, because it will save considerable amounts of time. You may also want to read these tips from

Business News Daily to use the product more efficiently.

CONTACT US IF YOU NEED HELP

Tracking your finances is very straightforward once you understand the basics. However, many businesses can't commit the time needed to learn or practice sound bookkeeping principles.

For business owners in all over the world, please do not hesitate to contact us if you are interested in our virtual bookkeeping services. We look forward to hearing from you.

BUSINESS BANK ACCOUNT

Separate Business & Personal Banking

Money is only a tool. It will take you wherever you wish, but it will not replace you as the driver.
—Ayn Rand

OPENING A SEPARATE BUSINESS BANK account that is for business vs personal financial assets is one of the first steps you should take when you have your own business. It is very important to do so that you stay away from what is known as co-mingling of funds.

This is to ensure that you will not have any problems and will be more audit proof when it comes to doing your taxes.

ONLINE BUSINESS BANK ACCOUNT

I personally recommend setting up your new accounting for small business checking and savings accounts with online access as this is the most convenient method.

This is especially true if you have the kind of job that keeps you on the go, out and about, or at multiple job sites.

You will need to make sure you have first established the kind of business structure you plan on running your new company under.

Make sure to go to the IRS website and get a new Employer Identification Number for your business type as well as a business name as the bank will want this information when you sign up.

ONLINE ACCOUNTING SOFTWARE

You can organize your business finances quickly and easily with online accounting software such as the most popular and well known one around, QuickBooks.

Bookkeeping & financial software allows you quick access to everyday tasks like invoicing, bill tracking, check-writing and payroll.

It is possible to track sales and expenses, share your data with Microsoft Excel and your accountant at any time. The online versions are great for ease of passing information between you and your bookkeeper also.

Plus it will allow multiple people to be able to access the information at the same time from different locations for virtual and remote work relationships.

You can even save time completing routine tasks and paperwork that will enable you to spend more time on doing the tasks you really love to do in your business.

ONLINE ACCOUNTING APPS

There are many different Apps available now that can help you organize and track your deductible business expenses as well as many different merchant service providers that can help track your income.

The greatest thing about these are that most provide an option for you to download straight into your accounting software and will even remember prior tax categories for income tax deductions and creating financial statements.

·

BUSINESS SKILLS AND BOOKKEEPING SERVICES

Three Critical Accounting Strengths

With the new day comes new strength and new thoughts.
—*Eleanor Roosevelt*

IF YOU ARE ASKING WHAT BUSINESS SKILLS and bookkeeping services have to do with each other, then you are asking a great question that it is time to answer. Many years ago during an intense conversation with one of my mentors, she advised me to always remember that there is only one constant; and that constant is that everything around us is changing.

That is so true. You just have to think of all the changes to the tax code every year to realize why I, as an Enrolled Agent and bookkeeper, providing tax and bookkeeping services, regard continuous learning as one of the most critical business skills and bookkeeping services for business owners and business professionals.

Can you imagine using the bookkeeping services of a bookkeeper who are not up to date with all the latest deductions you and/or your business can claim…?

One of the websites I frequently visit to learn more from posted an infographic that captured my attention. The infographic by Graham Winfrey listed the 10 most important business skills for 2020 as identified by the top then online colleges.

This got me to sit down and think what I regard as essential business skills and bookkeeping services for business owners - from my experience of working with them over the last 20 years.

And, though I came up with a lengthy list, for today's blog I want to narrow it down to three areas that I deem critical to business success.

3 CRITICAL ACCOUNTING STRENGTHS

1. *Intrinsic or Self-Motivation*

Intrinsic motivation can be defined as follows: "Intrinsic motivation refers to behavior that is driven by internal rewards. In other words, the motivation to engage in a behavior arises from within the individual because it is intrinsically rewarding. This contrasts with extrinsic motivation, which involves engaging in a behavior in order to earn external rewards or avoid punishments."

Intrinsic motivation is also defined as "The undertaking of an activity, as a hobby, without external incentive; also, personal satisfaction derived through self-initiated achievement."

Another definition is "Stimulation that drives an individual to adopt or change a behavior for his or her own internal satisfaction or fulfillment. Intrinsic motivation is usually self-applied, and springs from a direct relationship between the individual and the situation.

It is very important factor in the design of a training course.

From the above definitions and my own experience I regard intrinsic motivation as one of the most important business skills and bookkeeping services a business owner or business professional must provide.

Another way to think of it is: fueling one's own fire." As you all know, business is not always easy. There are competitors, technological challenges and changes, new legislation, etc. And, they sometime occur all on the same day...

To cope with all of these circumstances it is critical for a business owner to be self-motivated. To have a clear vision of what you want to achieve is great. To have clear and measurable goals on how to achieve your vision is outstanding.

But if you do not have the motivation to achieve your vision and goals, that beautiful vision and great goals are of no value. As they say, this is where the rubber hits the road...

My question to you: *Do you motivate yourself to achieve your dreams or do you need someone or something else to motivate you?*

2. Continuous Learning

I have already referred to it above. As business owners and business professionals we must have in-depth knowledge of our professions. We have to be regarded as experts at what we do. In other words we must be able to both "talk-the-talk" and "walk-the-talk."

As a bookkeeper I realized the value of being regarded as an expert. Not only do I make sure that I read a lot, I also studied further and qualified as an Enrolled Agent. This gives me specialized knowledge regarding taxation and allows me to represent clients in front of the IRS.

Another tool that I use to further my own knowledge and those of my clients is through blogging on my website. Blogging helps me to address the issues and problems that my clients experience on a daily basis.

And, every now and then I'll receive a question that asks of me to dig deeper into an unfamiliar area, thus helping me to broaden my knowledge and increase my value to my clients.

Remember, we all want to work with experts. And, when you are an expert, prospects and clients will come back to learn more as they have now embarked on the journey of "know, like, and trust."

3. Well Organized

Although I can talk in length about being organized, Dictionary.com refers to is as follows: "Having a formal organization or structure, especially to coordinate or carry out for widespread activities."

And, though there are many important areas in business to be organized, for me the most critical area is organization through accurate and up-to-date bookkeeping or bookkeeping services rendered by a professional bookkeeper. Keeping track of and properly organizing your business's expenses, income, account receivables, and accounts payable are essential practices for creating and maintaining a successful business. And, do not forget to add running and interpreting daily, weekly, or monthly financial reports.

Although many small-business owners may prefer to perform their business's daily and monthly accounting tasks themselves, experience have taught me that it is extremely challenging for business owners to execute successfully on both their business skills and bookkeeping services activities.

There is just so much they have to do to manage their companies successfully. When they have to add all the accounting activities to their daily calendar it just doesn't get done.

Therefore, it is important to look at your bookkeeping and organize it into activities that belong together and may make it easier to keep track of your business expenses, liabilities, and outstanding payments.

BUSINESS ORGANIZATION

Regardless of the size of a business or the business activity, it has to keep detailed records of its financial activities as it has to give full record of it every year end.

To keep it organized here are a few suggestions.

1. Bookkeeping Systems

Essentially there are two bookkeeping systems: single-entry and double-entry, which businesses can use:

- **Single-Entry Bookkeeping System**:

The single-entry bookkeeping is a simple system more suitable for personal finance. An example is balancing your checkbook.

It is regarded as single-entry bookkeeping as it involves a single account (checking) that is being debited and credited.

- **Double-Entry Bookkeeping System**

A double-entry bookkeeping system is regarded as more appropriate for business as it tracks two accounts at a time.

For example, when you sell a product in a double-entry bookkeeping system it records the transaction as a credit in the cash account, and a debit in the inventory account.

2. Professional Skills and Services

It is no secret that most small business owners lack the time, knowledge and experience to keep a detailed set of financial records. Two solutions to consider are:

- Using bookkeeping software
- Using the bookkeeping services of a professional bookkeeper.

If your business is fast paced, operationally complex, and dependent on precise and timely financial records, you should definitely consider using outside professional business skills and bookkeeping services.

How do you know when to engage the services of a professional bookkeeper? Consider it if the following scenarios are applicable to your business

- Your business keeps a large or sizable inventory
- Your employees perform billable work on client sites
- Sales may exceed $100,000 this year?

If any of these scenarios pertain to your business it may be in your best interest to get professional bookkeeping services as soon as possible.

3. Record All Financial Activities

Whether you outsource your business skills and bookkeeping services to a professional bookkeeper or keep it in-house, it is good financial discipline to keep track and record all of your financial activities.

4. Understand Financial Statements

Again, this is all about keeping it organized. Your bookkeeping software will help you to not only categorize your balance sheet and profit and loss statement financial activities, but also make it intelligent, or shall we rather say useable...

Consider the following questions:

- Do you know how much inventory you purchased last month or over the last quarter?
- Can you estimate how much business tax you'll pay next quarter?
- Can you forecast sales?
- Can you generate a list of non-paying customers?

The answers to the above and other related questions come from categorizing and understanding your financial activities.

Now your bookkeeping efforts will pay off as it gives you more insight into your cash flow and financial management.

SUMMARY

The above skills are from my perspective three of the most important skills business owners must possess.

I'm under no illusion that we will all agree on this and therefore I would appreciate your input in sharing with me what other skills you deem important.

BUSINESS PLAN ADVICE

Tips to Automate the Bookkeeping

The best advice I ever got was that knowledge is power and to keep reading.
—David Bailey

BUSINESS REVENUES SHOULD INCREASE significantly over the years. Unfortunately, higher revenues can create challenges for many business owners.

According to a recent study from The Institute of Financial Operations (IFO), many businesses are struggling to keep up with the growing volume of invoices.

The good news is that there are many ways that businesses can automate their business bookkeeping and accounting for small business.

AUTOMATE BOOKS

Charles Darwin once stated "It is not the strongest or the most intelligent who will survive but those who can best manage change." Darwin's quote is certainly applicable to the accounting profession.

Accountants are forced to handle a growing number of accounts, but few of them are looking for ways to improve efficiency.

Ken Brown, the executive director of the IFO, said that their unwillingness to adapt is creating a massive backlog for bookkeeping services and accounts payable professionals.

He said that even though many invoices are prepared electronically, the majority of bookkeeping and accounts payable professionals enter the data manually.

A surprising number of small business owners still receive paper invoices. Brown said that 27% of businesses receive 90% or more of their invoices on paper, while only 9% receive an equivalent number of electronic invoices.

BOOKKEEPING TIPS

Here are some automated bookkeeping tips every bookkeeping and accounts payable professional should consider.

Use Optical Character Recognition

Optical Character Recognition (OCR) is a technology that can pull data from invoices and copy it to other files.

Free OCR and Cuneiform Open OCR are among the best tools on the market.

Business Computing World reports that these tools can reduce manual data entry by up to 80%.

Take Electronic Images of Invoices

Businesses can use bookkeeping business software such as DIS-Imaging to take pictures of employer invoices.

This is an ideal solution in instances where the recipient of the email isn't responsible for processing payment.

It also makes it easier to store invoices electronically so they aren't lost in the future. Companies can further improve efficiency by investing in an OCR as well.

Look into Mobile Apps for Invoice Authorization

Most organizations require department managers to authorize accounts payable invoices before they can be sent.

These policies can cause the accounts payable process to grind to a halt if the manager is traveling or unable to respond to invoices.

Fortunately, there are a number of great invoicing apps worth looking into. Harvest, Paymo, Fusion Invoice and Paper Free Billing are all free apps that can streamline the process.

Consider Electronic Payment Options

A growing number of businesses are starting to pay invoices via electronic payment gateways. Paypal reports that 106 million individuals and businesses have started business accounting and it processes over $315 million in transactions every day.

The allure of electronic payment services is becoming increasingly clear. Businesses can use it to complete accounts payable much more quickly.

They can request that their customers send electronic invoices and pay them in less than a minute by logging into their account and clicking a button.

Paypal also stores records of all invoices, which can be exported to a CSV file. This drastically reduces the time involved in the accounts payable and accounts receivable process.

INCREASE EFFICIENCY

Every business needs to seek new ways to improve efficiency. The recent study from the IFO reveals that an astonishing number of businesses still don't realize how much time they waste not handling their business skills and bookkeeping services.

They may be able to improve their bookkeeping efficiency by 80% or more, which will be crucial as their volume of invoices grows.

They should find new ways to automate their bookkeeping when they reevaluate their business. Please don't hesitate to contact us if you are interested in automating your bookkeeping and we look forward to hearing from you!

SMALL BUSINESS TAX SERVICES

Finding Money Saving Solutions

*Focus 90% of your time on solutions and only
10% of your time on problems..*
—Anthony J. D'Angeloe

SMALL BUSINESS TAX SERVICES CAN HELP entrepreneurs save considerable money. They will be even more valuable if counties approve new initiatives to make new tax credits available to them.

Are you interested in taking advantage of them? The Sonoma County Economic Development Board is trying to expand the tax credits available to local businesses.

They have introduced some new tax credits that were made available under the

California Competes bill, which was passed by Governor Brown two years ago.

Under the new program, accounting for small business owners in all cities would be eligible for up to $31 million in tax credits.

However, many companies may need the assistance of local tax preparation services to navigate the new systems.

SMALL BUSINESS TAX SERVICES

A number of factors are stimulating the Sonoma County economy. These factors include the release of Pliny the Younger, warmer weather and the growing craft beer industry.

However, the positive impacts from these factors could be temporary, so small business owners will need to pursue more long-term plans to maintain growth.

The new tax credits the Economic Development Board has proposed will be enormously valuable for them.

Sonoma County Economic Development Board Program Manager Tim Ricard is confident that many local businesses will benefit. Ricard said that the subsidy application only takes a few hours to complete.

"You can possibly get $50,000 for a few hours' work," Ricard told *The Press Democrat*. "That's a pretty good return."

Several businesses have reportedly already received these benefits. MAC Thin Films Inc. was approved for $100,000 in credits over the next four years if it meets job creation requirements.

However, many small business owners may struggle to complete this documentation. The Economic Development Board hasn't released many specifics about the requirements, so it is safe to assume that many entrepreneurs will need to the assistance of small business tax services.

BUSINESS TAX INCENTIVE BENEFITS

While you will need to request an application to see what the eligibility requirements are, some of the details of the California Competes tax credit are available on Governor Brown's website.

Here are some of the requirements that Santa Rosa businesses must be aware of:

- The tax credits are available to California businesses that intend to expand.

- Approximately a quarter of the funds are available to small businesses with revenues under $2 million, so these businesses may have an easier time receiving funding.

- Businesses should demonstrate a commitment to paying fair wages to their employees, because the bill tends to give preference to such employers.

- Companies that receive letters of support from local government officials are more likely to be awarded tax credits.

The funding is available to businesses in any industry that want to grow in California.

Companies in emerging industries are definitely encouraged to apply for the California Competes tax credits.

If you would like to apply for the tax credits, then you should try to learn as much as possible about the initiative.

You should either speak with the Sonoma County Economic Development Board or an accountant that offers small business tax services. They can provide more details to assist you.

BUSINESS PLANNER

Functional Daily Life Organizer

One way to organize your thoughts is to tide up, even if it's in places where it makes no sense at all..
—Ursus Wehrli

BUSINESS PLANNERS ARE A MUST FOR everyone whether you have a business or not. Have you ever been one of those people to use a daily planner? If not, you should be.

As much as we'd like to admit, one of the shortcomings of being human is that we can't remember everything.

I'm a business owner and a mom, and with all of the different meetings in addition to field trips & athletic games, it's hard to imagine my life without a planner!

When you are in charge of accounting for small business, a business planner is a must. However, you don't have to be a business owner or parent to find a use for a planner in your life.

BUSINESS PLANNERS FOR ALL

There are many moms and independent business contractors who use planners to keep track of important dates and client information to have within arm's reach to reference back to.

So to all of the business owners or employees who only rely solely on your brain, or the calendar in your cell phone; it's time to stop!

If your cell phone dies, or the awful chance that you misplace it without backing it up to the iCloud, you will lose all of
that valuable information in the blink of an eye!

Save yourself the hassle, and invest in a hard-copy planner that organizes all of the new incoming information. It can easily be edited and updated, and in the long run, save you extraordinary amounts
of precious time.

FUNCTIONALITY

Find a daily business planner that is functional for YOU. If you get one that is too big or too small, you will begin to not like it, and find ways to never use it again.

Find one that is leather-bound (for the professional businessperson), or one that has a zippered enclosure so that all of your receipts aren't falling out (for the parent who does it all).

Whatever works for you, make sure that your life planner possesses that important quality, and you will be much more excited to open it up and use it!

USE COLORS

By incorporating a color coded system, you will be able to differentiate between doctor's appointments, business meetings, play dates, and other important tidbits of information within your professional planner.

If you can't bring yourself to using colors, use stickers instead. Stickers are really easy to find and come in all shapes and sizes.

If you are unable to find stickers that are the right fit for your planner; make your own!

By personalizing your very own calendar sticker system in your life planner, you will be better able to prioritize your activities months in advance.

BOOKMARKS

Make sure you bookmark the current date of wherever you leave off from day to day.

By using either a ribbon, or a handy-dandy butterfly clamp, you can quickly get to the current week and jot down
a small memo that you need to remember for later.

That way, the next time you open your organizational planner, you will fall right on that page you left off at, and can read the that important note you wrote for yourself to see.

GETTING STARTED

Now that you have acquired your very own personal planner, and have written down the important upcoming events, you have in your hands your very own personal assistant!

By having one that includes a calendar at-a-glance, has individual days (with ample lines and space), and either a color-coded or priority-sticker system, you will find that a planner is one of the best ways to organize your time and your life, so that you can be stress-free and find much more productive uses for your time.

> *If you enjoyed reading this book, I'd appreciate it if you would take a couple of minutes to post a short review at Amazon. Intelligent reviews help other customers make better buying choices. And because I read all my reviews personally, they will help me to write better books in the future. Thanks for your support!*

ADDITIONAL RESOURCES

www.Bookkeeping-Basics.net/accounting-definitions-glossary.html

www.Bookkeeping-Basics.net/accounting-definitions-wordsearch.html

www.Bookkeeping-Basics.net/accounting-definitions-ecourse.html

www.facebook.com/HorneFinancialServices

www.twitter.com/hornefncl

www.pinterest.com/hornefncl

www.amazon.com/-/e/B07HNKM6GK

www.smashwords.com/interview/hornefinancial

Accounting For Small Business Copyright © 2018 by Stephanie Horne.
All Rights Reserved.

No part of this book may be reproduced in any form or by any electronic or mechanical means including information storage and retrieval systems, without permission in writing from the author. The only exception is by a reviewer, who may quote short excerpts in a review.

Stephanie Horne
Visit my website at www.Bookkeeping-Basics.net

Printed in the United States of America

First Printing: October 2018

ISBN: 9781726636643

NOTES

www.ingramcontent.com/pod-product-compliance
Lightning Source LLC
Chambersburg PA
CBHW030454220526
45464CB00006B/2532